HAIKU

Harry Thomas

HAIKU

Harry Thomas

2020
Un-Gyve Press
Boston

Designed by Un-Gyve Limited

Manufactured in the United States of America

FIRST EDITION

10 9 8 7 6 5 4 3 2 1

Library of Congress Control Number:

2020941428

ISBN:

978-0-9993632-3-2

Un-Gyve Press is pleased to offer HAIKU also in a limited, signed edition with a number of the poems translated into Japanese by TAMURA Nanae.

Every hour the bell
In the Catholic belfry
The pine is heedless

Slender cypresses
A Roman poet called you
Candles of darkness

O eucalyptus
So many limbs lopped from you
How do you survive?

The flowers falling
From the jacaranda paint
The patio blue

What is that tree called?
I asked. Oh, an olive tree
But non-fruit-bearing

A hummingbird sips
From the spathe of the Giant
Bird of Paradise

Standing in their nests
Do the herons see themselves
In the bay below?

Armada Terrace—
Dozens of bees are raiding
The honeysuckle

The pepper tree at San Fernando and Kellogg—An Arcimboldo

My neighbor's pine tree
Is easily the best thing
About my neighbor

Last night in a dream
I kicked somebody so hard
I woke myself up

The small boy I'd find
Writing in grand mal seizures
Is now 62

The old woman says
It hurts to walk with a cane
To pick up a cane

In all its brilliance
The wisteria says
Get ready to die

Covered with blossoms
From the bougainvillea near him
The stone Buddha laughs

The dew on the grass
Is morning dew on the grass
I think of Issa

How large the crow is
Flying up from the branches
In the evening breeze

The koi in the pool
Listening to the rock singer
Know it's not Japan

Every time I feel
Cutting back the rose bushes
Is a desperate act

The camellia tree
As white in its pale clay pot
As a summer cloud

I regret picking
And not picking the thyme leaves
And rosemary sprigs

The avocados
Green globes on the neighbor's tree
Are just out of reach

From the age of four
I learned more than you would think
About suffering

Through binoculars
The cars moving on the bridge
Seem barely to move

Ants in the kitchen
Struggling like the rest of us
To go on living

The rapacious owls
Rest till dusk in the tall trees
Above tiny skulls

The white-haired woman
Raps on the watermelons
With bony knuckles

The coyote lopes
Down the street in the evening
His ribs prominent

As the rain comes down
You can feel the summer heat
Leaving your body

In the lobster tank
The banded lobsters seem dead
Or to be dreaming

Afternoon shower
Line of ants scurrying down
The magnolia trunk

The heron's strange voice
A silent era actor
After the talkies

The green hydrangea
The cold water I give it
Goes straight to its head

A woman goes by
In a sailboat her blonde
Hair in the water

A ship in the fog
A long wail from her whistle
Announcing she's there

Walking to the store
Women carry umbrellas
For falling sunlight

On my wife's nightstand
The photo of her father
Is bigger than mine

Higher on this hill
Richard Henry Dana climbed
Bundling firewood

Reading an old book
I find a worm on a page
Been on it for years

The parakeets sing
In the outdoor screen cages
Until the cat comes

In Sydney I saw
The evening sky black with bats
Fleeing fireworks

The Ocean Beach Pier
Whole families casting lines
Into black water

The restaurant
Is so well-tended the birds
Go elsewhere to eat

June—cloudy all month
Now on July 1 sunlight
Illumines the house

Lightning bugs vanish
A Japanese haiku theme
But they have vanished

Where do you belong?
I asked the dog. Then he seemed
To ask the same thing

A ballerina
In slow motion, the egret
Fishing the shoreline

The owl alighting
On the eucalyptus branch
Doesn’t bring the night

The summer solstice—
Spent the day longing for snow
In Massachusetts

The summer solstice
I commend myself to you
Despite everything

Sitting on a rock
The dog gazes intently
At the dark water

No, Buson, moving
Frequently from house to house
Did not keep me young

That slip of a palm
Was the first one of my trees
To die in the drought

Get out of the way,
You crows, some crazy drivers
Are right behind me

Impenetrable fog
The seals barking on buoys
Watery beacons

As a child I loved
Seeing it hang faint and still
The afternoon moon

The lavender-blue
Boat-shaped spathes fill with water
For the local birds

The Siamese in heat
All night the neighborhood toms
Crying out in need

Men are disgusting
They argue just to argue
Women not so much

Melville saw it too
This tortoise butting against
Immovable things

Where did childhood go?
Even from these photographs
It has disappeared

It's Bon-Odori
I'll light a lantern for you
My dear brave mother

The dead bamboo stalks
White and leafless and rootless
In a grove of green